70

PRAYERS AND SONGS

to

GOD

DEANNA SMILEY

WESTBOW
P R E S S®
A DIVISION OF THOMAS NELSON
& ZONDERVAN

Scripture taken from the Holy Bible, NEW INTERNATIONAL
VERSION®. Copyright © 1973, 1978, 1984 by Biblica, Inc.
All rights reserved worldwide. Used by permission. NEW
INTERNATIONAL VERSION® and NIV® are registered trademarks
of Biblica, Inc. Use of either trademark for the offering of goods or
services requires the prior written consent of Biblica US, Inc.

WestBow Press books may be ordered through booksellers or by contacting:

WestBow Press
A Division of Thomas Nelson & Zondervan
1663 Liberty Drive
Bloomington, IN 47403
www.westbowpress.com
1 (866) 928-1240

Because of the dynamic nature of the Internet, any web addresses or
links contained in this book may have changed since publication and
may no longer be valid. The views expressed in this work are solely those
of the author and do not necessarily reflect the views of the publisher,
and the publisher hereby disclaims any responsibility for them.

Any people depicted in stock imagery provided by Thinkstock are models,
and such images are being used for illustrative purposes only.
Certain stock imagery © Thinkstock.

ISBN: 978-1-5127-1787-7 (sc)
ISBN: 978-1-5127-1786-0 (e)

Library of Congress Control Number: 2015917909

Print information available on the last page.

WestBow Press rev. date: 10/26/2015

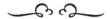

Fear of the Lord is wisdom, and to shun evil is understanding. Seek the Lord with all your heart and with all your mind, and you'll find him—I promise. You'll find him because I have.

Lord, you're the author of man. You know his comings and his goings, his every thought. So why does man continually lie, steal, cheat, and take innocent lives as if no one sees—not even you?

Lord, you see and know everything. How foolish can a mind become? Does it decay with time? How sad. Time teaches and develops, or so it should.

How patient you are, Lord. But how long will you be so patient? I know you'll destroy wickedness someday.

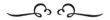

I promise you, Lord, from this day and forevermore that I'll live like the new creation I became the moment I received Jesus Christ as the Master of my life.

What do righteousness and wickedness have in common? I'll separate myself from every evil and unclean thing. I'll live for your strength, help, and righteousness. I won't give room to the Enemy. I'll stand firm, and I'll triumph over every evil that tries to subdue me. You're my Lord and my unseen eternity.

Lord of my life, I owe you a million prayers. Millions of thank-yous. Millions, my Lord.

My breath is yours; you own my mind. With a willing and grateful heart, I surrender all that's in me. Teach me, my Master. Lead me, guide me, and show me your ways.

I commit my life to you. May the work of my hands be pleasing to you. I can't function apart from you. My every prayer to you is, "Without you, Lord, I'm nothing."

Lord, we don't praise you enough. We don't thank you enough. We don't love you enough. We don't give you enough honor and glory.

The world should be crying out to you in thanksgiving because you haven't destroyed us. You did destroy the first world. We're wicked beyond words.

Lord, I want to tell you how much I love you, thank you, praise you, and worship you. I honor and glorify you. Thank you for your patience with this world.

Your love does endure forever. You're an awesome God, worthy to be praised.

I've lost count of all the times I've come to you in my distress, dear Lord. Yet you've always answered, time and time again.

This world loves those who belong to it. I'm in a world I don't belong to. You, Lord, are my refuge, my safe haven. I trust you with everything. I wait patiently for your messages.

You promised never to forsake me or leave me. I'm not afraid. You said not to fear, for you're with me. I love you, Lord. I trust you. I adore you.

Dear God,

I do have a thankful heart. I know how wonderful you are. I know how many prayers you've answered for me. I'll continually praise you.

A thankful heart brings victory. I'll bless your name with gratitude and thanksgiving. I'll sing to you, God. I'll sing to you with a grateful heart.

Thank you, Lord, for daily making my burdens light.

Praise the Lord! Praise the Lord!

My life has been anything but simple and easy. Dull? No!
Boring? No!

I've been busy living and learning, loving and teaching,
laughing and crying, working and playing.

Lord, you're the never-changing, never-ending, constant
force in my life. You're my strength, my shield, my shelter
in all my storms.

If it hadn't been for you, Lord, I wouldn't have remained
strong, steadfast, determined, dedicated, and overflowing
with love.

Thank you, Lord, for being here for me. I do love you.
Truly, I love you.

My God, I know that you know every secret, good and bad, and that you'll judge everyone someday.

The broad road is still the one most traveled. Eyes are forever closed to the truth. Hearts are hard from selfishness and greed. Minds refuse the truth because it interferes with the road most traveled.

I know my duty, and I'll praise you. Loving and giving are my gifts from you.

I'm eternally grateful for your mercy toward me. How can I thank you? Let me count the ways.

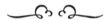

I praise your name forever, Lord. My heart is yours alone.

Lead me, Lord, for each step I take and every choice I make. No turning back, Lord, no turning back. Rescue me, set me in your presence, and be my stronghold forever.

My dreams, my hopes, my will: let them all come from you and you alone. I acknowledge that I no longer live, but Christ lives in me. I'm a vessel **of** honor.

I'm totally and completely yours, Lord. No one comes before you.

Many have tried to steal me from you, but they have tried in vain. You're still my first love, and you always will be my first love.

I exist to please you. I compete with your many other loves, for I know you've shown me favor.

With all my heart and all my mind, I'll spend all my life loving, praising, and thanking you for being my true love.

We give thanks to you, O God.

You've saved us from the Evil One. You've been our shield throughout our life journeys, a constant help and hope for our tomorrows. Without you, we wouldn't exist.

We're ever giving praise and thanksgiving, for we know who saves. We know to whom we belong. We'll confess you to the people. We'll praise you wherever we go, for great is your love, and great is your faithfulness.

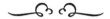

When we follow you, God, you won't allow us to fail.

We're cracked and broken vessels, full of selfishness and every sin.

We think you should follow us and answer to our every whim. Bless me here; bless me there. Bless me; bless selfish me.

You, Lord, are first—you and you alone. Obedience to your Word, meditation on your Word, and surrender to your will bring victory for our lives.

Victory over sin and victory over self. If we follow after your heart, victory will be yours.

Lord, why are my greatest enemies the ones I have given the most to? The ones I've prepared for, cared for, dined with, walked with, talked with, fellowshipped with, and nursed in sickness in their wounded states? Why do they become my enemies?

I know you know the reason, Lord. Only you can know the heart.

Count my tears, Lord, and count the years. All day, Lord, they twist my words and watch my every move. They truly want my life, but I won't be afraid. I give my enemies to you, Lord, because you'll be my shield.

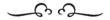

How many ways can we call you, Lord? How many names do you answer to? In how many ways can we reach you? I've heard of quite a few. No matter the name, Lord, I love them all and call you them often. You're sometimes called "the great I am"; the Lord is who you are, the God who always was.

The self-sufficient God.
The unchangeable God.
The self-fulfilled God.
Much revealed, much hidden.
The Lord: that's who you are.

When I'm afraid, Lord, I'll trust in you. When my enemies attempt to devour me, I'll remember your words. I can't forget your promises.

You're an awesome God. You'll surely send your angels to surround me. You're an awesome God, an ever-present source of every good thing. What can man do to me?

I've made vows to you, Lord: I'll always serve you with all my heart and all my mind. I'll keep your words in my mouth. I'll meditate on them day and night. I'll sing praises to you—day and night, I'll sing.

Lord, just to be close to you always—that's my desire. I want to be in your presence, to know and feel your reassurance.

My love for you overwhelms me. You've stolen my heart completely.

When I wake up each morning, you're my first thought. Praise and thanksgiving form in my mouth. You're so worthy to be praised.

You're my comforter, my joy, my peace. You're my strength and my perseverance. Always, Lord, meet me in our secret place. I adore you, Lord. I adore you.

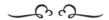

Holy, holy, holy Lord God Almighty. So awesome, holy, and righteous. No man can see your face.

Holy, holy, holy, the Most High God, Creator of the universe. You're the strength of your people. You're the God of glory. You make yourself known, the end from the beginning.

Before you, Lord, every knee shall bow, and every tongue will confess your name. You're holy, holy, holy Lord God Almighty.

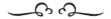

I know you're with me in my walk, dear Lord. You have been from my beginning. You knew me in my mother's womb.

Thank you for knowing and loving me, and thank you for predestiny.

Thank you for your Holy Spirit.

Thank you for Jesus, and thank you for the blood.

Thank you, Lord, for walking with me, talking with me, and hearing me when I call.

"No one who practices deceit will dwell in my house; No one who speaks falsely will stand in my presence" (Ps. 101:7).

God Almighty, I know how much you hate lying lips. Lying seems to have no end. One lie opens the door for many more lies. Once put into motion, a lie can become a tidal wave.

Lies can affect one life or many lives. Broken lives, broken homes, broken hearts, lasting pain—Lord, create in us a clean heart. A false witness won't go unpunished.

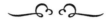

I love you, Lord, and I humble myself before you. I beg forgiveness for my sins.

I know you love me, and I know what you expect of me. With all my heart, I live to please you.

My adversary, the Devil, fights hard to steal me from you. The struggle is real; the struggle is fierce. Strengthen me and forget my offenses.

I'll fight with your words in my mouth, your Spirit in my heart, and the sacrificed blood of Jesus on my hands. I'll stand firm and fulfill your purpose for my life.

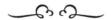

You are my heart, my joy, my peace. You are an awesome, almighty God, so full of love, compassion, and forgiveness. You loved the world so much that you gave your only Son as a living sacrifice to save the world from eternal damnation.

You promised to always be with your people in troubles, trials, and triumphs. You promised to love us, deliver us, and show us your salvation. You are awesome, you are almighty, and you are God!

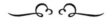

Almighty God, Creator of everything that is, was, and ever will be! Your Word says, "No man can look upon my face and live." Cover me, Lord, and allow me to feel your presence, your wonderful presence. Speak to me through your Word.

I eat, drink, and sleep while meditating on your Word. I love you, I adore you, and I worship your holiness. Your Spirit keeps me safe. The world threatens me, but your Spirit keeps me. Nothing can separate me from thee!

Attack on America
September 11, 2001

Dear Lord,

I am not confused about the attack on America. I know that we are not alone; there are worlds and heavens beyond our sight. There are spiritual powers of darkness and evil. Satan, man's accuser, is constantly seeking whatever he can steal and devour.

Satan stole some hearts that day, and many people died!

Above all else, guard your hearts, for hearts are the wellspring of life. Pray always (Prov. 4:23).

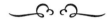

All Scripture is God breathed, and the hand of the Lord is majestic in power. Each time my burdens grow too heavy to carry, I give them to you, my Lord.

You are my help, my shield, my warrior, my every good thing. I am not afraid; you have done great and wonderful things. I know who I am, and I know whose I am.

My peace, my hope, and my joy are you, Lord. I will be glad and rejoice in you, my Lord. Always my Lord, always!

Dear Lord, I'm positive that you despise selfishness. Unselfishly you gave your only Son to save the world, because you loved us so much.

Selfishness is sinfulness—me, me, me, and everything for me. What a wasted life to live. Selfish ones will never know what a joy it is to give. Selfishness is ungodliness, and giving is living. What a joy it is to live. Lord, redeem the selfish soul.

Praise the Lord; praise the Lord; praise his holy name; hallelujah, hallelujah, hallelujah to the Lord. Nighttime and daytime give praises to the Lord. He is worthy; he is worthy, worthy to be praised. Bless the Lord, bless the Lord, and bless the name of the Lord. Lift him up, adore him, worship him, and magnify his name. He is awesome, and he is love; praise his holy name. Praise him daily, keep his laws, and let him know you love him. Blessed are you, Lord. You give life to all.

This is a hurting and a dying world. We suffer, Lord, because of our sin. We don't give honor, we don't give praise, and we don't seek your face. Sabbath worship is not true worship. When we humble ourselves, fall on our faces, and repent of our sins, you, Lord, will show and give your goodness and mercy, and we will know that you are God and that there is no other. I know you are the God of mercy, the God of love, and the God of forgiveness. Forgive us, Lord, and love us and show us your great mercy.

After all, you made us in your own image and likeness.

Dear Lord, if only I could stand before you and greet you face-to-face. "No one may see me and live" (Ex. 33:20). Cover me, Lord, the way you covered Moses. Oh, that I may see you and behold your glory. All I want is more, Lord, more of you. Every word of instruction, every breath, every chance for another tomorrow to praise, to glorify, to adore, and to worship you—those are all my heart desires.

All I have, all I am, is yours, Lord. I love you, I adore you, and I praise and worship you.

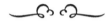

Satan's time is short.

He is angry and desperate.

He's full of wrath.

His target is everybody.

Children, old men, young men, old women, young women.

Any cracked or broken vessel is his for the taking.

Lord, this is my prayer: strengthen your people and give us power and endurance that we may stand immovable until the end. Breathe on your people, Lord, so that we become renewed like eagles. May we shout out in praise and thanksgiving in loud and mighty voices.

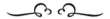

Heavenly Father, my thoughts trouble me. My enemies are relentless; they attempt to consume me day and night. Their eyes cut like a knife. They spread rumors and make threats. I am suffering unmercifully; my heart is broken beyond repair. Horror has taken hold of me. In my despair, I cried to you. Please rescue me and hear my prayer. Surely you are my refuge; surely you are my strength; surely you will deliver me from all my troubles. Deliver me, Lord, from this dry desert place.

Heavenly Father, I call to you in the name and authority of Jesus. I am your servant, and I submit to your will. Lord, in the power of your name and through the sacrificed blood of Jesus, I ask you to shield me and deliver me from this evil that has come against me. With you as my source, I stand against anger, violence, depression, oppression, abuse, lying, and every sin.

Holy Spirit, give light to my path and liberty to my mind and my spirit. Help me to show love through my words and deeds. And grant me your righteousness, Lord, through Jesus, I pray.

You, Lord, are the One, the only One, the Way, the Truth, and the Light. Lead me, Lord. I will follow; you're the center of my life. All of my hope is in you; your way is my way.

I bind my mind to your mind; you are my destiny. Your Spirit fills me with truth and revelation. Thank you, Lord! Bless your holy, holy, holy name.

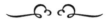

Lord, I know I can trust you totally, and I can depend on you. I can love you totally and know that you love me totally. People love is maybe love. Your love, Lord, is truly love. Your Word is a constant comfort and strength, a beacon of light in a world of confusion.

I know why I love you with all my heart. I know why I seek you with all my soul. You are unchangeable and everlasting.

My Lord, I know you have a purpose for everyone born.

The Devil too has a purpose; he has plans to destroy your plans. This is war—real spiritual war—on the earth.

There is your will, Lord.

There is the Devil's will.

There is man's free will.

We as your people must put on the full armor every day. We must prepare ourselves, for this battle is real; so is the Enemy.

I promise to keep up the battle as long as I live. I will never surrender to the Enemy's will.

Our Father, you are all power. "Is anything too, too hard for God?"

There is nothing you cannot do. And for those who love you and keep your commands, there is no good thing you will withhold.

I love you, Lord. Give me your peace that passes all understanding. Give me your Spirit; he leads to knowledge and truth. From you and through you and to you are all good things!

Wonderful Jesus, you loved us beyond words; you came to die for us. You walked with us, prayed with us, and taught us things God taught you.

Jesus, I love you, I adore you, I worship you, and I magnify your name. "The name above every name." I long for you, Jesus. Stay near me and always keep me in your prayers to our Father. Never leave me, Jesus. Never, ever leave me.

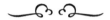

God, above all you said to attend to your words, to keep them in the midst of our hearts. Teach us to meditate on them day and night. May we observe and do according to all that is written. Lord, I know you work only through your Word; you are magnified by your Word. If I stand by your Word, you will stand by me. I have set my heart and my eyes on you, Lord. Thank you for being my Savior and my Lord.

Forgive me, Father, for I am a sinner. Please accept my shameless begging. Attend to me, Lord; wash me in the cleansing power of the blood of Jesus.

Fill me with your Spirit; fill my lips with sweet morning and evening prayers.

Thanksgiving and praise are in my mouth. A song of trust is in my heart. Forever I love you—forever, my Lord!

Dear Lord, my iniquities have separated me from thee.

Now your face is hidden from me, and you will not hear me. Hidden away somewhere in my heart is secret sin. Search me, O God. Know me, try me, and see me.

Show me what displeases you. I will renounce the sin and put it away forever. Without you, Lord, there is no me. I always want to be pleasing to thee.

I have set my heart to find you, Lord. Nothing will keep me from thee. My ears eagerly await to hear from you; my heart quickens at the thought of you. I feel no need to eat or drink. Your Word is all I need. It's written on my palms; it's burning in my heart. I place sweet prayers on my mantel to let you know just how I feel.

You are my most high and loving God. Lord, command your angels concerning me and show me your salvation.

Lord, with a broken heart I cry. My mind is filled with pain and fear—pain for me and fear for my children.

Lord, I cry with a broken heart. In bitter anguish, Lord, I cry. You know my beginning and my end. Unless you rescue me, Lord, my enemies will devour me.

Does he who knew me in my mother's womb not hear my desperate cry?

Make haste, my Lord, and rescue me. Make haste, dear, dear Lord.

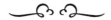

Lord, I know you work only through your Word, and I meditate on your Word day and night.

My very first words to the morning light are, "I love you, Lord."

Open my eyes and open my ears that I may learn wonderful things from your laws. Lead me, teach me, and guide me in your way.

My Lord, at the end of my life, let me dwell in the shelter of your shadow. Lord, show me your mercy and give me your love.

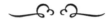

So long, Lord, I have known you. So long, Lord, I have loved you. Constantly I seek your face. When I was a child, I called to you. You have been my closest friend, and you have taken all my sins.

I will declare to all I meet the wonder of your ways. Until my end someday, my Lord, your love for me will guide my days.

Lord, each day I pray. Please be my safe place, my strong place, my comfort, and my peace. I have completely surrendered my life to you. Where you lead, I will follow.

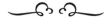

My Lord, my Lord, do I cry in vain? Do you hear me, Lord? Do you love me, Lord? I know you know my name. What stops you, Lord? What keeps you silent?

Did I somehow hide some sin? Some very secret sin? Search me, God, and know my heart. Do not be far from me. You are my hope, my strength, and my promise of purpose. Do not be far from me. Forgive me and cleanse me and love me, Lord. Please hear me once again.

Since my youth, O God, you have taught me and kept me with your grace. You put a shield around me, Lord, and made sure my enemies lost their way. What love you've shown me in my life there's no way I can repay.

I just want to please you, Lord, to give honor, and to obey. I will love and serve you all my life. You are more than I deserve. Please, Lord, stay with me and guide me every day.

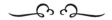

I am troubled, Lord, deeply troubled. Please come to my rescue. Weeping and mourning overwhelm me. My enemies attack constantly. All night I prayed, and I cried. My troubles consumed me; I moaned in my agony. I grew weak and weary in my wait for you, Lord. I cried for strength from my unseen source. Draw near, dear Lord, and let me live. Give comfort through my tears.

Dear Lord, you are my refuge and my fortress. You are my strength in my troubles. You are the Light in my darkness, the cure for my ills. I could live a thousand years with just the two of us. I close my eyes with thoughts of you and praises to your name. When I awake, my first recall is, "Did I say his name?" You're near me, God. I know you are.

I feel your love, and your love, Lord, is better than life.

To know God is to love God. To love God is to honor, obey, trust, praise, glorify, thank, and wait upon God.

Praise the Lord, O my soul, praise the Lord. Glory to you, my Lord. Glory to you forever. For being God alone, we thank you, thank you. We honor you. We love you, and we wait on you forever.

We give you our praises—praises for day and night, for strength to rise, for freedom to choose, for the earth itself, and for people to cover it.

Lord, you and I know I am a sinner. Forgive me, wash me in the blood of Jesus, and give me your salvation. I surrender, Lord, totally to you. Your will is my will. Apart from you, I am nothing. I will follow you all my life.

Give me understanding to guard me and wisdom to teach me and save me from the ways of the wicked.

Children are the future, Lord. They are our future, your purpose.

Satan, the ultimate liar, steals, kills, and devours. Lord, have mercy on those in most need of your mercy, the children. Be patient, Lord, loving, and kind. Always in your infinite wisdom we know that sin and corruption are still the root cause.

Evil angels grow stronger each day. But your angels and your power can wipe them away. Children are so worth saving, their love so worth having. Send angels, Lord, to show them the way.

Children!

So many are hurting, innocent, and small—so not guilty.

Abortion! Abuse! Abandonment! Such horror. Lord, I pray with fervent prayers; day and night I pray. Send your mercy and guardian angels to keep them safe in the midst of sin and evil.

Lord, you are mighty and strong. Lift up your voice and send out a shout, a command to the angels, to subdue the evils that destroy the children. Lord, lift up your voice. Please!

Fear not! Never will I leave you; never will I forsake you (Heb. 13:5).

I know your promise is real. I have been delivered from the depths of the grave. I am committed to you, Lord; there is no other. In my darkest hours, you were the only Light for me. You calmed my fears, and you dried my tears. Step-by-step, day by day, you showed me every right way.

My Lord and my God, bless the mothers who love the children. Bless the hands that gently hold, bathe, and feed them. Bless the voice that soothes and sings—and, when it's time, teaches and scolds. Bless the mother who truly loves.

Keep her, Lord, patient and strong, generous, kind, understanding, and demanding.

Keep her righteous and pure; keep her focused on you.

Bless the mothers who show the world the love the Lord has shown to all.

Lord, you are amazing, so amazing. You keep me strong in every storm. You walk with me, you talk with me, and you show me the way. You are truth, and you make truth known.

Amazing grace—you give such amazing grace. I have been brought to my knees in anguish and pain over and over again. You've come to my aid and helped me to rise time and time again.

Thank you for being my amazing grace.

"Our Father in heaven hallowed be thy name thy kingdom come, thy will be done, on earth as it is in heaven" (Matt. 6:9–10).

Father, my heart knows not what words to use to beg forgiveness and seek mercy from you for me and my family.

Lord, in the name of Jesus, send the Holy Spirit to teach and guide and speak through me that my prayer may be acceptable to you.

Fill my heart and mouth with your righteousness, Lord. How do I ask you to rescue and heal me? Holy Spirit, teach me.

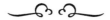

Dear Jesus, my name is Jerrell, and I am only three months old. I can't talk! But my grandmother puts words in my mouth—words like "Jesus loves you. He is sending angels to watch over you. You are very safe. Never be afraid. Jesus is always looking out for helpless babes. No harm will come to them." Grandmothers beg so shamelessly every day and every night.

Dear Jesus, I'm three years old, and my name is China. I have been told about you. You brought the gospel. You came to heal us and show us what love is.

You came to tell us about your Father and your Father's will. I'm glad you came. I'm glad I know your name.

Heavenly Father, I want to praise you and thank you for giving me the heart to live, the heart to give, to love, and to grow. This world is cold and very hard. I know I'm an alien in this foreign land, but my strength is from you, Lord. I know whose I am. Thank you for family and friends. Thank you for your grace, for it has made me loving, loyal, supportive, understanding, and real. With praise and worship I magnify your name. With love and adoration I lift you up. Thank you, Father. Thank you.

How did you save me, Lord? Why did you save me? Was it because you loved me so, or was it because I loved you so? I've seen so much I could have become and so much I could have done. You saved me, Lord, from so much sin! It's amazing what you've done. I've always known I heard your voice, so I listened, Lord. I think that's why you saved me. I listened!

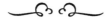

Our children need you, Lord. We have lost too many through the lies of the Enemy. Lord, from you come wisdom and knowledge. Give mothers and fathers a double portion of your wisdom and knowledge. Keep them always a step ahead of the Enemy. Lord, stop Satan from his slaughter of the young and the innocent. Give us your mercy, Lord, **as** we pour out our hearts to you with our thoughts and our prayers.

Lord, protect the lives of your children's children.

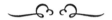

Trust and obey! There is no other way. You proved your love for your people. My Lord, you gave your only Son to save the world you created. When we surrender to you totally and love you completely, there is no good thing you will not do for those who love you.

Thank you, Lord. Thank you for your love and your Word. Thank you for Jesus; thank you for the Holy Spirit. I adore you, I lift you up, Lord, and I magnify your name.

Lord, bless the fathers who walk the walk and talk the talk. Bless the fathers who hold the hands and grow the man. Bless the fathers who hear the whines and take the time to soothe the tears. Bless the father who waters his seed and watches it grow with love and attention.

Bless him with strength, honor, and endurance. Bless the fathers with long lives to see the fruit and savor the blessings of a life well spent.

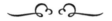

Lord, Lord

Let me sing a song for you and tell you how I long for you. I can't begin to understand how anyone can live without you.

Day and night you're on my mind. I'm ever thinking how to find another moment with you, safe and secure from all earth's harms. Teach me how to walk with you. You are God and God alone; no one compares to you.

Let me sing a song for you.

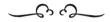

El Shaddai

The almighty God. The God with all power, no matter how big the problem. It doesn't get too big for God. He has said, "Is anything too hard for God?" I confess your awesome power, Lord. I obey, and I honor you. I have courage. I know you will do whatever your Word says. I know you perform mighty and wondrous works. You are the all-almighty, all-powerful ruler of the universe, El Shaddai.

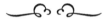

Jehovah-Tseboath

The Lord of hosts, you are a warrior and a winner of every battle you undertake. As your people, we are to follow your lead, to take our place, to put on the full armor, and to go into battle. This fight is the struggle of our lives, for it isn't against flesh and blood but against spiritual forces of darkness and evil.

Lord, you stand; we stand. You conquer; we conquer. With our faith in you and with your Word in our mouths, we will stand, we will fight, and we will win with our Lord of hosts, our Jehovah-Tseboath.

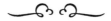

Jehovah-Shammah

The Lord is there, always. In sickness and sorrow, you, Lord, are there; in poverty and wealth, you are there. And in joy and in pain, Lord, you are there in our loneliness. Your Spirit is speaking to us, letting us know you are there.

You love us and show us favor. You give power and strength to your people.

"We sing praises to you, Lord." We glorify your name.

"We love you, Lord. You are there, always."

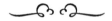

Jehovah-Tsidqenu

The Lord is our righteousness; many of us are blind to God's righteousness, numb in our sinfulness, and therefore committed to evil—lying, stealing, murder, hatred, wrath, and idolatry. Until we know and confess that we are earthen vessels and cannot live righteously apart from you, God, we will fail.

Only when we totally and completely surrender to you will you begin to work in our lives and lead us to your purpose. You will show the reason for our being. You will show us your righteousness.

Jehovah-Repheka

The Lord is our healer. If you diligently obey the voice of the Lord, do that which is right in his sight, and keep his commandments, he will heal all our diseases. God always keeps his promises. We have to keep ours. God needs more praise, more love, more honor.

We are spoiled and forgetful. We remember God when we need something. Jesus went to the cross, suffered, and died for our sins; and by his stripes we are healed. When we act like it, talk like it, and pray like it, we will see it! Hallelujah!

Jehovah-Jireh

The Lord will provide; the Lord provides everything the followers of Jesus will ever need for spiritual battle in this world.

Time and time again, I have received the perfect Scripture for the problem at hand. The Holy Spirit has led me to the perfect place, where I've found the perfect book. Friends and family call with a word of perfect prayer and encouragement. Lord, you are always opening doors, books, and mouths; and yes, Lord, you do provide.

Jesus Prays for Himself
John 17:1–5

"Father, the time has come. Glorify your Son, that your son may glorify you. For you granted him authority over all people that he might give eternal life to all those you have given him. Now this is eternal life: that they may know you, the only true God, and Jesus Christ, whom you have sent. I have brought you glory on earth by completing the work you gave me to do. And now, Father, glorify me in your presence with the glory I had with you before the world began."

Printed in the United States
By Bookmasters